Necessary Lessons to receiving your Blessings

It Was

All

Necessary

VANESSA M. CARY

It Was All Necessary

Necessary Lessons to receiving your Blessings
Published by Vanessa M. Cary

Copyright © 2023 by Vanessa M. Cary
ISBN print: 979-8-218-16454-6

Disclaimer

All the information in this book will be used only for informational and educational purposes. The author will not account for any results from using the contents herein. While conscious and creative attempts have been made to ensure that all information provided herein is as accurate and valuable as possible, the author is not legally bound to be responsible for any damage caused by this information's accuracy and use/misuse.

Every attempt has been made to source all quotes properly.
Cover Art: Victoria Ross
Cover Design: Victoria Ross
Formatting and Interior Design: Brandon Evans
First Edition 2023
Printed in the United States of America

TABLE OF CONTENTS

Acknowledgment

My sincere gratitude goes to my mentors- without whom my journey would have been fruitless.

My special thanks go to Keenan Williams and family, Sparkle Marie, Derrick Grace the 3rd, Will Woundtree, Myron Golden, Sunny Lenarduzzi, Justin Phillips, Grant Cardone, Coach Stormy, Shawn Blanchard, Mike Kimbrough, Rebecca Garrett, Runway Billionaire, Neo Davi. You have all been immensely part of my success story, and I appreciate you.

DEDICATION

This book is dedicated to my four sons, Nigel Jr, Nisear, Levi, Jahar, and my father, David A Cary Sr.

They have been my motivation to keep going on in this life. My goal is to ensure they have everything they want and need. I will ensure they are left with property, land, and wealth. I do not know where I would be if it were not for my sons.

In memory of my baby sister Cheryl Green My Father David A Cary Sr, Shaquana Watson, and my baby niece Tahliyah Taylor

PROLOGUE

It may seem paradoxical that I, whom several people emulate, should have come from a comfortable middle-class home. Yet to a remarkable extent, I created my epitome of doctrine that says, "Our socio

economic circumstances condition us." The States where I grew up gave me a sense of long historical tradition and, simultaneously, close contact with the grim realities of the underdevelopment then characteristic of my environment.

My subsequent inability to have the stable life that every average individual should have heightened my alienation.

I was born in Long Beach, a large community of about eleven million inhabitants, consisting of a diverse number of odd Californian guys and one of the loveliest - situated as it was in Long Beach,

surrounded by vineyards and luxuriating in almost Mediterranean greenery.

My sons are inspired to pen my life experiences. I was inspired to tell my story because it can help many people.

I was starting from my fight toward leaving a toxic relationship where I lost myself. What I gained afterward has been so wonderful and fulfilling. From the lessons, I found myself and gained my confidence back. I left a toxic relationship, embraced spirituality, and, most importantly, began my entrepreneurship journey.

The purpose of this book is to encourage people who find themselves in difficult situations like mine - If I could do it, yes, they can.

You are strong enough. Everything we go through in life is for a reason. You are designed to learn and grow. So, leave behind whatever brings out the worst in you. Stop ridiculing yourself - don't lose your essence. There is no point in turning to the people who hurt you for help. Whatever you wish to do in this lifetime, you can always do it.

Change toxic habits and do things differently to get a better outcome. Change your mindset from a poverty way of thinking and think bigger and better about yourself - your spirituality. Speak positively to yourself and watch what you speak about yourself. Invest in your knowledge to progress. You must think and talk differently if you want to change your life.

I had to self-evaluate myself- why am I attracting these people? It had to be me.

I had to find myself again and regain my power as a woman and Mother. I started to self-reflect and realized I had much to work on.

This has changed my life for the better in a significant way. We are what we speak. So, I began to talk about nothing but positive things about my life. One day, I thought I wanted to write a book and start a business. I knew I was cut out for it because I worked many jobs and learned much from them. My story will motivate someone to leave a toxic relationship, have a spiritual awakening, or start a business.

As you read on, I hope you also understand that Pain, growth, and other lessons are necessary to fulfill destiny.

Chapter 1

MY CHILDHOOD YEARS

All the shit I had to experience before I got here. Tough times never last.

My name is Vanessa M. Cary, and I was born into a family of four (4), three girls and a boy, of which I happen to be the eldest daughter and the second oldest child of my Mom. My eldest brother is 13 months older than me, and I have two little sisters behind me.

My parents are separated, so my Mom had to pay the bills alone. I guess, as a single mom, she did her best. This has taught me to take up responsibilities from a tender age to assist my Mom in catering for the home.

At age fourteen, I started work, and my first job was in the summer, where I worked with the YMCA at

Wilson Park. It molded me into the person I am today. When I was younger, I always had a strong work ethic. I love to try new things. I used to cheer and dance in high school. I was just very outlined; I like to be around people, and I'm an all-around people person. I want to help people; if I know something that my friends or family do not know and is beneficial, I will try to help them.

I can be a good teacher or life Coach, too, because I like to get out there and research; I do not want to go off of what was told to me my whole life; I love to do my research and then find my answers and do my own thing.

I was so independent, hardworking, and determined to set a good example for my little sisters behind me so they could look up to me. It made me a humble, strong, and ambitious young woman who got involved in many jobs. I love learning new things and trying new things, and I am the type who never wants to depend on anyone for anything but

always aimed at being an elder sister, one that her little sisters would always and forever look up to.

Unfortunately, I lost one of my little sisters, Cheryl Green, on December 15th, 2006. She was murdered at a friend's house around the corner from where we lived. She just so happened to stop at one of our family friend's houses in the neighborhood. She was shot at while trying to save herself from the Hispanic gang's gunshot, suddenly starting from nowhere. Eight persons were outside about that time, including a two-year-old boy; they were all African American.

My Mom and I were the only ones at home when Cheryl's best friend came bearing the sad news that my little sister had been shot right in front of the driveway. My Mother and I rushed to the hospital; unfortunately, she died there. Of the four people who got shot, she was the only one who didn't survive. That occurrence alone changed me a lot. I still feel like that moment has made me who I am today regarding my ability to keep going, no matter what I go through or what obstacles happen.

I had to go out there and show the world who I was and what I had to offer. I will get to start my business and author my book; I want to teach my kids- this was how I had to motivate myself to start a business and do whatever I wanted. If I could do it, then you can do it too!

Yes! We all go through stuff in life. It's a part of life. I remained and moved forward because losing people close to me made me resolve to change my family's

dynamic and break the generational curse. I want to do something different. I want to leave my kids' homes and wealth. They didn't ask me to be here, so I will teach them everything I know to have a prosperous life.

My Mom owns nothing, property or assets, and my dad doesn't. Unfortunately, my father was murdered in Las Vegas, Nevada, on January 15th, 2023, and he didn't even have life insurance. So I don't have anybody to look up to or motivate me in my immediate family. Everything that I have been doing in my life so far, I went out there to do on my own; I Am going to break that limiting curse. Once I started working at 14 years old, I have been working ever since. I probably took a few breaks here and there, but for the most part, I kept a job. Subway was my first permanent job at 16 years old. I loved it. I felt independent and responsible for myself. I had my share of doing shit and getting in a bit of trouble, but nothing significant.

I was doing my own thing. I worked at four different Walmart's and have done almost everything in the store. I can run my store from everything I've learned, from the Walmart job to the Tax preparing job. Yes, I also worked at Liberty Tax Service as a Tax preparer. I even got my CDL driver's license and drove school buses which I didn't like. Those shits are enormous to be toting around. I feel like I have done it all. When I put my mind to doing something and visualize it and believe it, it is so and will happen. You have to feel and know that you can accomplish it. So don't have any doubts. Growing up, I never said I wanted to do taxes, but I learned and did it. I got promoted to level 6 at Walmart: supervisor of over 30 + associates. Who would've ever thought? But it showed me what type of worker I am and how I manage under pressure. I did it all, and I'm glad that I did.

Chapter 2

THE MEN IN MY LIFE

I never had it good with the men in my life either. It wasn't easy with the fathers of my children. Sometimes I wonder if something was wrong with me, or was I just unlucky?

My relationship with one of them was the most turbulent. I met him in 2016 when my 3rd son Levi was just ten months old. I was 27, and he was 40, about 12 years older. He walked into my job one day. I was working at Walmart in his military uniform at the time, and he introduced himself. We exchanged numbers and started talking. We didn't regularly speak at the start, but our communication deepened and became frequent later.

Six months after we met, everything was cool. I didn't see any signs of a mental disorder. Then, one day after our first meeting, he told me about how he walked in to buy something at my job at Walmart one day and went off on a customer. He was in the line to pay for items he picked, then snapped at a guy because he was standing too close behind him. His rationale was that he wanted the guy to give him some space. I bought the story and his reasoning and never imagined what that meant for our relationship. So, I didn't ask myself serious questions - is this how he flares up at the slightest provocation?

As we got into the relationship, in the beginning, everything was good. It wasn't perfect, but it was manageable. We would go out to eat a lot with the kids. At that time, I only had three kids, Nigel, Nisear, and Levi was the baby., We took them out to events and did a lot of stuff like normal and happy families do.

In 2018, when I moved in with him and got pregnant, the relationship began to have cracks. I noticed a meaningful change in his attitude. Things worsened when the pregnancy was about three or four months. He started having trust issues and would cut off my phone plan because we used the same phone plan. Toward the end of the relationship, I had to get my phone line because I got tired of that. I had a friend at the time,

Porche, and we would go to chill and play bingo. He became so jealous of my friends. Sometimes when I was at bingo, he would text to accuse me of doing all kinds of despicable things and send me and Porche paragraph after paragraph. Mind you, and I never gave him nobody's phone number. He would get them online because I was under his phone plan. When I got home, the situation escalated into a big issue. His rage of jealousy and escalation at home became a vicious cycle.

One particular day, I went out to play. I was about four or five months pregnant with my last and final son Jahari. He kept calling my phone. I was tired of his frequent calls and had to block him before it got overwhelming. He switched to texting, and I also blocked him. When I returned to my car, he had packed five or six bags of my clothes and some of my stuff out of the apartment. I went to get in my car, and all my items were scattered inside my car. He had access to my car keys because he cosigned the vehicle. So, while I was playing bingo, he came up and did what he did. I had to properly arrange my stuff in my car to sit and drive to my sister's place because I was not going home that night.

So, I got to my sister's place, where he was already waiting for me. I had briefly told my sister about the situation before I got there. She didn't tell me that he was there. He came out from behind the door waiting for me when I walked in. Why are you here? Did you get here? I asked. I never gave him my sister's address. He must have been tracking me. How could you treat me that way and pack all my stuff? I asked a million questions. He felt terrible right after he did what he did and came to my sister's house to apologize. That was the first significant incident between us, and I knew deep down that I needed to leave. Things would only get worse from here, I said to myself.

I couldn't leave immediately because I had to find a place, but I was pregnant and earning only a disability allowance to support the family. He was working, so he took care of the rent. I focused on my unborn child. So, I just had to play my cards right. I had to wait for the right time when I could afford to have a roof over my head. My Mother knew some of what I was going through and wanted to help me. I moved out from my Mom's place at 19 years old, right after I had my 1st son Nigel Jr and never returned to being a burden on her, especially after having children. My Mom offered me a Section 8 housing voucher to me as a way of help because she didn't need it. She was just about to get remarried and stayed with her fiancé Alvin. She told me I had to find an apartment quickly if I wanted to take over the voucher. Otherwise, the voucher would not be valid anymore, and she would let it go. I knew I needed to leave this man before I ended up on the First 48, so I searched until I found something. I came across a lovely two-bedroom apartment in East Long Beach, California. This was also around tax season, so I had the money to move in. I was so grateful for being able to find something for me and my boys to live and not have to deal with the madness anymore. I was ready to leave after my Mother paid for and signed everything. One day he went to work, he worked the graveyard shift from 4 am to 12 pm, and that was my cue to go. I called my Dad and Mom, planned a date to move, and asked for assistance just in case he would show up while I was moving, and he did. Despite him showing up, we still packed all my shit and left. I was done with the relationship; our son was about 11 months old.

Afterward, I left him and rented my apartment. Now that we are apart, the behavior has gotten worse. He still texts me all kinds of evil shit a man shouldn't say to the Mother of his kids. I guess he's upset that I left and has been bitter about it, and he constantly accuses me of cheating on him or having outside influence as to why I left him. He doesn't seem to understand why I left. I gave him a chance. I sacrificed, and I moved in with him. I tried to make it work, tried couples counseling even had another baby for him, but things worsened.

Chapter 3

I Overlooked the Red Flags

P
ay attention to everything, and don't let shit slide. I was a little vulnerable and not paying attention to things I should have. Though all I have been through has made me a stronger woman, I wish I was more aware of red flags and paid more attention to actions.

We have to pay attention to certain things to avoid certain problems. For example, I would have avoided that whole drama if I had paid attention to things like anger, temper tantrums, and some of the shit he would say.

The lessons I will share with you were learned the hard way. Being number one, do not ever go by appearance when you meet people. Looks can be deceptive. Judge people by their actions. You have to spend time with them and take notice of changes in the mood and atmosphere when something occurs, like a typical disagreement. Nobody's relationship will be perfect, but how your partner reacts can tell you much about them. You must know yourself, pay attention to your intuition, and watch everything because everybody is different and could have childhood traumas or mental challenges. I suggest that you do not rush into anything. You should date for at least three years before moving in with someone. If there is one thing I do know is to take time and get to know them before taking a big step and moving into someone's space or vice versa. Energy never lies.

I cannot say that I regret it because I have an awesome baby. I passionately believe that everything happens for a reason. All my kids are here for a reason; they are my only blessings from my relationships. I've been on my own for a while now, and I realize that the more you're on your own, the stronger and more independent you become.

You can survive whatever relationship challenges, but watch out for the signs. The most crucial symptom is mental abuse. You must know when to walk away because you can't stay in an abusive relationship and get something good out of it.

Leaving can be challenging, but you can do whatever you want. But first, you must know you can and will do it and not let anything or nobody stop you. A mindset shift has to occur for that to happen. Next, you realize that we must reprogram ourselves, mainly our minds, then nothing can stop you from achieving your goals.

Figure out how and what you want your life to be like, then plan and visualize it in your head. Plant it in your brain and water the thought every day. I bet you it'll grow. Then, take action daily, moving forward towards that picture/vision. I have been through many things that should have weighed me down by now, but I'm still standing strong and determined to win.

A mentally ill person can do anything if they can't control their emotions and actions. If he pushed me today, he could punch me the next day. It is those "little" things that lead up to big things. That little stuff can be emotional, physical, or mental. It's all the same. It's negative energy.

He would call my Mom and sister to discuss our issues badly. I would never do something like that to him. I believe they are issues we can resolve between us. We don't have to involve families. I would never call his Mom or his daughter to talk about him.

We tried couples counseling. I'll never forget when he admitted to the counselor that he does things intentionally to get a reaction out of me. Who does that? He is a retired veteran, and I never knew he was diagnosed with PTSD, bipolar disorder, schizophrenia, or all that stuff until we moved in together. Then I saw all his pills, and he had appointments with his therapist. He doesn't take medication; our cabinet was full of medicine. I felt for him, but that doesn't excuse his bad behavior. At the height of our relationship drama, I was mentally drained and often felt sad. Sometimes I felt sorry for myself, and it led to depression. I felt tired and wanted to move on.

I knew I had to leave him. I got a CDL school bus driver's license for a better job. I've always been determined to succeed, so I worked hard. I didn't have any of my sons to put their dads on child support. I had them for me and told myself I would always care for my boys the best I could. This book I'm writing, and this business I'm starting is because of them, so there are no child support arrangements. I don't want to keep them away from their father, and do my best to maintain healthy boundaries with them. My oldest two boys live with their father, and it's nothing wrong with that. People will try to judge or look down on you because your benefits or situations are better than theirs. As long as the children are fed, being well-mannered and having both parents is always a blessing. And fuck what anybody negative has to say about it. I've experienced this, and I didn't let it break me.

Chapter 4

I Gotta Keep Going

I'm not giving up when I've come this far.

I am very independent and try to do my best as a mother and not depend on anybody else. That's how I have always been.

After getting pregnant with Jahari, I couldn't return to Walmart because I didn't particularly appreciate how I was treated there. Before maternity leave, I was a warehouse supervisor, and the job was highly stressful. That was when I decided to do the training for my school bus driver's license. So, I became a bus driver for a little while before COVID-19 happened.

The lockdown never stopped my dreams.

I'm trying to start a business, write a book. I stopped sharing my dreams with people because nobody would support me the way I supported myself.

I decided to put all the drama behind me and focus on the beautiful future ahead of me. I want to build a big house with everything for me and my babies.

With a movie room, a basketball court, a park outside, a backyard with a swing, a sandbox, and a slide for my babies. I want our house to be comfortable and made just for us.

My dream is to be financially free - to pay my bills every month on time with no problem. Though it's been hard, I want to be able to push money into my business.

I've been learning everything possible about starting a business to have a good life for my family. They don't teach it in school. Nobody taught me about generational wealth, how to create wealth, manage my finances and savings. Life will be different for my children. They will not have to start a summer job at 14 years old to earn some money. I brought them into this life. I should be able to get them whatever they need and provide for them.

They will not struggle because I started off struggling at a young age. I had to work because my Mom couldn't meet my needs. Instead, she made me pay bills at about 15 years old. I should be able to

keep the money I was working for, but that never happened. My Mother should have encouraged me to save some. I'm just learning how to save a little. I have an EIN, LLC, Website, logo, etc., for my business. I would be a fool to stop now. I have been learning on my journey. There is so much information out there that school doesn't teach us. Investing in my mindset and myself has been a game-changer for me. I will keep investing in myself and information until I'm old and can't read anymore. I also had to learn not to overwhelm my brain. It is not healthy for you to overwhelm yourself with information. Trust me, find one thing and master that, then you can branch off to the next. I swear it was like I was learning a new skill every week and not giving what I learned previously to manifest. Something new does something to me, significantly if it can help and benefit me and my family. Investing in a $20 to $60 course is easy and quick. I paid $900 for a credit repair service and just now saw results a year later, but that purchase was worth the wait. When I first purchased my LLC, I had no idea what to do, how to structure it, nothing. It cost me $5 in California to file my LLC, but I didn't know all the other shit that goes with it. For instance, I didn't know that you should never tie your personal phone number, email address, or address to where you sleep as your business address. It wasn't until I found a mentor about business credit on TikTok that I realized I had to start my LLC all over. I ended up paying for information and found out how to obtain a business virtual address, email, and phone number. These are mistakes that I have made. I want to help others who want to start a business and give them the best advice and information possible so these common mistakes will be avoided. I made a lot of errors, but it's ok and all a part of my success story. My so-called Mother decided to put me and my kids out of the Section 8 apartment. It threw me off because she had just remarried. My goal from the moment I moved in was to get my place under my name. It's all a part of why I also wanted to start my own business. I never wanted to be in a situation again where somebody could put me and my kids out whenever they felt like it. I have no relationship with my so-called Mother because I just got fed up with the treatment, especially when I'm not around. Ever since I moved into that apartment, I felt like she was plotting against me and didn't help me from the kindness of her heart but only helped talk about me to others and held it over my head forever. So, because things weren't going her way or I wasn't kissing her ass, she put me out. I hated it when I was little, and my Mom got upset. She goes and calls the whole family, telling them what I did. My siblings and I hate this about our Mother; she has worsened as we grew up and started having family problems. I feel like a mother is supposed to protect her children from hate and negative energy. Mother should correct her child and be an example for her children. With my Mom, which isn't the case; she was always the victim and did shit wrong. I got tired of her bashing. I don't want any negative energy around me and my children. Even having a negative conversation about me and my children while I'm not around to defend myself is OUT. It's been too many times people have told me things my so-called Mother would say negatively about me. It's very hurtful, and I tried to have a genuine relationship but can't continue if there's no change on her end. Any relationship takes two people, not one person. I don't want anything else to do with her. Leave them where they are until a person can admit and own up to their bullshit.

Chapter 5

GETTING MY MENTAL HEALTH RIGHT

A strong person realizes the need to stop bad habits.

I used to smoke weed; I used to smoke cigarettes. I completely stopped all that. Changing unhealthy ways and improving every area of life is always good. I never tried to be a burden on my family. We all go through our stuff, and I don't want to add my problems to anybody else's.

I have decided to be strong. I can't let the urge for nicotine spoil my life. I want to live long for my kids, and

I need to be here to teach them and show them before I leave. I will leave a house, car, trust, businesses, and land for them. I'm teaching them everything I've learned in my life and experiences and trying my best to keep them from making the same mistakes I made.

I learned to breathe correctly and meditate because I started having bad anxiety. One day I thought it was over for me. I felt like I was about to die. How fast my heart was racing. I'm like, no way, I still have a lot of shit that I must accomplish. A bunch of people that I need to help, at least listen to, but I need to save myself and crack these codes before I can help others.

I'm 35 now, trying to elevate and get out of poverty. Here, without a poverty mindset, trying to build shit and make boss moves, so the enemy will not attempt to come in and knock me down.

I'm making all these changes in my life because of my kids.

The changes that I made have impacted me tremendously. I'm more focused on the stuff happening in my household and around me. I pay attention to how people treat me.

Now I meditate when I can, especially when it's quiet. I take my women's healthy heart and hormones supplements and herbs regularly.

Now, I feel better and more energized. I'm happier and more excited about my future because I know I have God, my Boys, and a bright future ahead of me. I have dreams, and I believe I'm going to accomplish them. Even Though the enemy tried to throw confusion and stop me, none of that would stop me. I'll continue to stay focused on my goals. I also write down my affirmations as much as possible. I have learned that other people's emotions and problems are not mine. Whatever they are going through has nothing to do with me. Some people will blame you for the way your life turned out. Protect your space and your peace. Energy has never been a liar. Listen to it and pay attention to your intuition. You are not our past. Whatever has happened in the past is not who you are today. Some fail to realize that people can change for the better. Just because you've done something ten years ago doesn't mean you will do it today.

Life is a different story for every person on earth. We all have different stories, struggles, family issues, mental challenges, etc. It is nobody's right to judge the next person because nobody is perfect, and we all have to go through what we need to go through to change and better ourselves. People will try to bring you down to a low vibrational frequency with them; I'm not having it. If I'm out with friends or family and something negative about another person becomes a topic of conversation, I will quietly exclude myself or not say anything. And some people wonder why drama always follows them. If you surround yourself with shit, it's destined to find you. I'm heavy on protecting my energy because I don't want to become bitter and angry. I won't want to hear it anyway. Let's talk about business ideas, or meditating is my kind of language. Once you realize that the words we use daily are spells, you wouldn't let anything anybody says affect you negatively. Most people sleep in the real world, and I plan on staying woke, so if that means cutting off certain friends and family members, be it. My peace of mind is way more important and should also be important to you.

Sometimes, we must cut people out of our lives, and it's ok. In my case, it's my Mother. I'm not allowing anybody to hurt me again in life. So, I'll keep her far away from me and my family. I went into hermit mode for a few months. I had to detox from all the toxins others fed me. All of you are not about to drive me crazy, is what I told myself, and from that day moving forward, I haven't let anybody bring me down to a low level. If I hadn't cut my Mom off, she would have made me so angry that my heart started racing. If anybody makes you anxious, you should stay far away. That negative energy they hold can jump onto you really quickly. Don't allow energy vampires to come and drain you out.

Chapter 6

MINDSET SHIFT TO ENTREPRENEURSHIP

I've always known that I had a more significant calling in life and to create a brand for my family. So, I'm not working for anybody anymore. Instead, I'm going to build my empire. It's been challenging to find people with a similar mindset, and that's why I have online mentors that I look up to and listen to. I get a lot of my information and knowledge from them. They are millionaire mentors who have built generational wealth for their families and are trying to help others.

I like to find like-minded people online because I don't have any people who vibrate at my frequency around me.

I started considering entrepreneurship because I wanted to change my life and that of others. I've lived in this property for so long, working and paying bills. I lived paycheck to paycheck and never had enough money to do what I wanted to do. But, as I mentioned earlier, once I break free from all that, I will help many people.

People will not listen to you if you don't have any money or accomplishments. So, you have to show your achievements somehow for people to listen. So, starting a business or becoming a life coach, a teacher, or whatever, ensures you are credible.

I know I have what it takes - worked since I was 14 and always received promotions in every job. So why not put my all into my own business?

Nobody in my immediate family has a

business. I will be doing something new for my family and myself. My entire family will benefit from my success. I can teach my family and friends all I've learned about business and the importance of investing in yourself. If they want to do it and learn, they can do it. It's a must that I am a role model to my siblings, my family, and my kids. Writing this book is perfect; I'm taking on entrepreneurship simultaneously, which will help me put my challenges and what I've experienced into the book.

I look forward to writing another book documenting my business success.

I never expected this journey not to be challenging because my life was always full of challenges, but I always overcame them.

When I was 18, I moved out of my Mom's house and have never returned. I never wanted to be a burden on anyone. I had to stay with a friend.

The reality is that we're all grown, and you can't keep running back to Mom.

I run a healthy living e-commerce store. I haven't made any online sales yet because I'm trying to get my website together and get more products. My products include Organic Sea Moss gummies, 14-day detox teas, and foot detox patches. I plan to add organic pads, tampons for women, and charcoal toothpaste soon. I also plan on launching a course or eBook about starting a business.

I've been making sales without even launching my business.

I will ensure I succeed in helping as many people as possible. I have to stay focused on the goal. I can't let other people drown me with their problems. That will not be fair to my kids and me. My last real corporate job was at Walmart in 2019. I left there as a Warehouse supervisor in charge of over 30+ associates. Every day was a new challenge, but I bet I never let that stop me from doing my job. At this same Walmart, I was promoted two times in 3 years. I learned how to work the register, supervise all cashiers, and deal with the many types of vendors that came to the store daily. It was a great work experience because I learned much from 1 place. The best advice I can give someone still working a 9-5 is to take everything you know from it and utilize anything helpful for your benefit. I'm taking everything I've learned from every job and will use it if need be. Invest in a course. I bet it will change your thinking and help you take a risk for yourself. We do it daily anyway with other shit that won't help us. Forgive yourself for your past mistakes. You are not that same person. Every day to me is a learning day. Do research online. YouTube is free. Give yourself at least 1 hour daily for your alone time and studying. It will significantly benefit you later. I have a toddler and a 7-year-old, and two teenagers. If I can do some research, then so can you. You are putting forth daily action toward your goals; eventually, you'll start seeing results.

Also, take care of yourself and your health. Health is absolute wealth. I'm big on taking your vitamins and drinking your tea every day. I promise you will feel a difference in how you show up for yourself. Things will prepare you for your journey; make these daily things a habit, a must-do. Like how we wake up, wash our face, and brush our teeth, that's a must.

Chapter 7

GOTTA INVEST IN PROGRESS

Scared money does not make you any; I had to invest in my mindset.

Once I started investing in myself, my life changed. I have learned more about business than I did going to high school for three years. I dropped out in the 11th grade, and now I know why I never really liked school. It wasn't ever fascinating to me, and other females didn't want me for some reason. I'm the coolest person, so I thought. Trouble always seemed to find me. I struggled in high school and wouldn't say I liked it. Finally, I bought a program by Keenan Williams. It is a fantastic program to help people start a business. The thing he teaches is that it is crucial to put your product out there. You must show up and out for yourself and your business.

He teaches how to start and grow a business; this involves marketing. I'm learning how to market to the world.

Keenan has made multi-million dollars just by doing that on his own. When he started promoting his skin care products, within his first year in the business, he made 3 million by marketing on Instagram.

I also invested in programs to get my mindset right. I needed to change the way I was thinking. I felt like my soul was missing something. That's when I came across information about mindset, meditation, spirituality, and self-awareness.

You will become a better person if you change the way you think. It begins with being open-minded. Another critical factor is the people you surround yourself with every day. You reflect on the people around you - especially those you regularly talk to or are around. So, the big question is - who are you communicating with daily? Are they negative or positive? You get positive energy from positive people and vice versa.

I learned that if you want to improve as a person or in business, you must also invest in your relationships. Meet and build relationships with people who know things you don't or can help you improve your life.

Some healthy food tastes good, while some are not very delicious, but we eat them regardless of their taste because of their benefits. You don't eat everybody's cooking, so you shouldn't consume everybody's energy. Some people will nourish your soul, and others will poison it. We also consume unhealthy foods because we like them or because they make us feel better. We should always do things that will improve our lives, regardless of how difficult it may be. It's been best for me to stop harmful habits and lifestyles, irrespective of how good they make us feel.

One of the most potent discoveries I made is that - regardless of the past, you have what it takes to create the kind of future that you desire. But you must put in the effort and invest in yourself to make it happen. We spend money on bullshit all day. Why not invest some in a course to learn a new skill or career? Anybody can do whatever it is that they want to do. But it would be best if you first believed; that is why our mindset is critical. It can be a trap for you or a launching pad to success.

You could spend $10 on an eBook to help you meditate or get a planner to help you write down your goals to plan stuff out. It's necessary to invest in yourself. Invest in it if it will make you smarter, wealthier, and more credible.

Just watch out for scammers, primarily online. I have been scammed and do not even like talking about it because I think back and want to kick my ass. Please be careful. Social media can be a danger zone. You have to research people and be sure they are credible before you invest with them. Don't just give your hard-earned money to whosoever piqued your interest.

We spend money on fast food, clothes, movies, and stuff that we can only enjoy for a short time, so why not spend money on something that can help us for the rest of our lives? There's some information out here that can change your life forever. I have spent over $5,000 on courses, credit repair, business coaches, etc., and I'm grateful I did. I remember paying $120 for my business's EIN and later found out it was free. Never pay for an EIN for your business; it's free on irs.gov. This has been a learning process for me being a first-time business owner. I've had to endure some setbacks and a lot of self-healing to finally accomplish my goals and dreams of being a business owner and helping others.

If you ever consider starting a business, I suggest you begin the process with an open mind. Then, get ready and be willing to put your all into it and change your surroundings. Get ready for a journey. I'm still in the process of building my brand. I will continue, build momentum, and not rest on my efforts., take time to find the reason why you want to start a business in the first place. Focus on a product or service that meets a significant need of your customers. If you are selling, make sure it is different and unique. Be yourself and trust the process; embrace the good and not-so-good.

Chapter 8

SEED MONEY

Finding seed money, being flexible, and working multiple side hustles to keep my dream of being an entrepreneur alive.

Every entrepreneur knows the importance of funding their business, especially the starting capital, often called seed money.

Just as I invested in my business and mindset, I did so to get my seed money or starting capital.

I invested in grant writing programs that assist entrepreneurs in writing business grant applications. They also help with funding for businesses. I paid $200 a month for two months., I have not been able to get any funding for my business yet, but the effort is worth it. I have always made sure to have some income coming in. One thing about me is that I'm a bingo lover. I like to play or work in a hall where I engage with everyone. I used to run my own bingo game every Tuesday afternoon, and I enjoyed it. Eventually, I stopped because I was putting more into it than what I was making. I help out at bingo halls. They call me the bingo caller, and I run the game. I usually get paid for it and receive tips from the players when they win. I can make pretty decent money if enough people are playing. I remember calling a whole bingo game, and I made over $500. There was a time when I would call five different games a week. I had to have completed at least $2,000 weekly from the five games because I was the only bingo caller. That was some excellent hard-earned money. Bingo will be something that I will always do, whether it be playing or working. It's something that I enjoy and where I can get some time. I only work on two games weekly because I focus more on my family and business. I even went and got a job at Amazon. It was through a contractor with Amazon to drive the vans and make deliveries. When I say I hated that job, I hated it. I had to do it for a very short time, like two months. It wasn't until I had a breakdown at work that I knew I had to quit. I had never felt so defeated by a job in my life. Everything isn't for us, and that job was not for me. I say protect your Peace and Mind with everything in life! My mind told me to leave that job before it killed me and then be replaced the next day. I was not about to go out like that. I like to try new things and jobs to see if it's for me or something I enjoy doing.

I will never give up on my goals and dreams. I didn't come this far to stop. My dream might not be as easy as I desired, but that's life. Starting a business without money and just with an idea is not easy. A lot comes with this, and you must prepare for bad days. It's not all peaches and cream, and some information is not given for free. You must be willing to sacrifice and invest in yourself. You need to pay for all the necessary documentation to do it correctly.

Despite the obstacles, I'm closer to getting proper funding for my business than when I started. And I won't give up till I get it. This is the message I want to pass on to my children and those who read my story.

You can't be scared to invest in yourself. Don't get discouraged, and ensure the person you're getting your information from is credible. I can't stress this enough, watch who you listen to or send your money to online. I would have been tight with my money and never invested in myself; I would not be where I Am today. All bullshit aside, investing in yourself can change your life if you put action toward it. It might not look like it initially, but it will manifest if you keep at it. If you work a 9-5 job, still dedicate some time to work on your dreams. Not long ago, I learned the importance of saving a little something. You should always have money for a rainy day if you have children because they always need something. Structuring my business correctly has been challenging, but I didn't let the mistakes I made stop me. I may have been at a halt sometimes, but I always got back to it.

Chapter 9

THE IMPORTANCE
OF PATIENCE

Being able to accept or tolerate delays and not letting little things get you angry or upset is all a part of patience. I had to work on it and am still working on it to this day. I have four sons, and every day can be a challenge. But I love challenges. I've had numerous delays on my journey; if I had let them defeat me, I would not be here telling my story and having only one parent tell me that I must move out of your apartment right after losing your other parent. His murder was unexpected, and I had to stop everything I did to get him buried properly. My father was a rolling stone, I would say. He had ten children with four different mothers. Out of all of my dad's kids, I was the closest to him. I just really understood my dad and knew he didn't know how to be a dad. He lost his parents at a young age, so he didn't get the guidance he needed growing up. I never met my grandmother or grandfather on my dad's side of the family. They both passed away before I was born. Pops didn't know any better and had a temper, which stirred my other siblings away from him. I would always see my father whenever he was in my area or if I was in Vegas, where he resided before his death.

I am very grateful for the time I spent with him and the memories I have of us on the phone for hours at a time. All I have said, the message in this book is incomplete without mentioning the importance of patience. Every good thing in your life worth waiting for takes time to manifest. Going into this new chapter in my life, I knew it would not be easy and quick, and I didn't think it would take almost two years to manifest. The reason being every situation meant to break me didn't. It may have stopped me then, but I always returned to it. It will be times when you don't feel like it. I've been there numerous times. You must eventually find the strength to get out of that state of mind and not let it overpower your ability to make shit happen. You can do it, always know and remember that you can. Never let bitter people, places, or things redirect you from your calling. If you do the work and work on yourself daily, then whatever you need to know will be revealed.

Don't get frustrated because things are not working out on your timeline. If you don't give up, everything will come together at the perfect time. Meditation has helped me keep my mind calm and free of cluttered and negative thoughts. I usually do mine at night before bed, but anytime during the day is good if you try. It can be hard to do if you have young children, but we are not making excuses here. Find yourself a spot and make it your own. I don't care if it's in one of your closets. We must take time for self-care, mind, body, and soul. I had to learn to meditate correctly because I didn't know how to quiet my mind at first. The more you do it, the better you become. It is free, and many teachers can help with meditations and affirmations. Writing down your goals and affirmations daily are good stress reliever and habits. I speak them to myself and write them down to manifest sooner. There is still so much for me to learn and master. I'm taking my time and putting what I've learned and been researching into action.

Do you ever feel like you're having anxiety?

Take a break. Stop whatever it is that you are doing. If you're not sitting, take a seat and try to calm your mind.

The most crucial thing in that moment is your breathing. Take a deep breath in, hold for 3 seconds, then release. It would be best if you did those ten times. That technique helped me tremendously. I had to stop letting what I'd been through stop me from my greatness. I know what to do and won't let fear hold me back. Be fearless, be kind, be you. Shine so bright that they can't see anything but light when you walk into a room. Know your potential and know your worth. Vibrate so high that the low vibrational one can never touch you.

You can only control your life and situations, not other people's demons and emotions. So, walk away from drama if it comes to you. We must start being the example we want to see in others. Always walk with your head held high and your light shining bright. Don't dim your light for NOBODY!!!!!

Chapter 10

OUR AFFIRMATIONS

The affirmations I will share are essential to me and my boys. Our parents are our children's first teachers, so we must start teaching and installing healthy habits in them at a young age. Then, kings will know how great and powerful they are. So, every morning, these are my boys' affirmations I have them say out loud.

I Am Strong.

I Am Healthy.

I Am protected and safe.

I can do anything I want to do in my life.

I Am a fast learner

I Am Confident

I Am Happy

I Am Loved

I Am worthy.

I do my best to install positive words in our daily activities.

Here are the affirmations I say and write daily.

I Am grateful for the family I have.

I Am Healthy

I Am protected and safe.

I Am Strong and confident.

I Am a successful business owner.

I Am a successful bestselling author.

I Am a money magnet.

I Am a multi-millionaire.

I have multiple sources of income.

I Am creating generational wealth for my family.

I Am breaking generational family curses.

I will be the 1st millionaire in my family.

I will help and teach others when in a position to do so.

I will give back and help others.

I Am creative and talented.

I will buy my dream home.

I Am financially free.

I can accomplish anything I set my mind to do.

I will never give up on myself or my dreams.

I will start multiple businesses.

I will teach my sons about financial literacy.

I Am successful in everything that I do.

I Am powerful, happy, loved, and grateful.

Say these to yourself or make up your own and notice how peaceful and fulfilling you feel. Meditating is another excellent way to relieve stress and clear your mind. I know I will help someone. Thanks for reading my story.

This is just the beginning of a young mother's long, fulfilling life journey going through life and learning as I go. In the process, I remain sane and stable to continue and finish what I have started.

MORNING CHECK IN

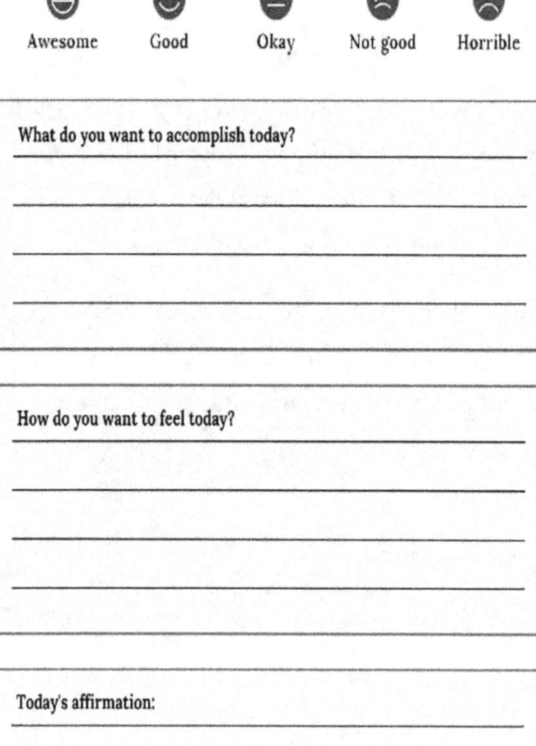

What do you want to accomplish today?

How do you want to feel today?

Today's affirmation:

 My Daily Gratitude Log 

Today's "my moments..."

I am "GRATEFUL" for...

Affirmation/ Quote of the day

5 minute journaling

5 minute journaling

5 minute journaling

5 minute journaling 

5 minute journaling

5 minute journaling

5 minute journaling

Me at four years old

*Me at nine years old with my dad
and little sister Cheryl on the side*

Me with my mom's children in 2006

My dad and I in 2013

My friend and I, Shaquana Watson, at her baby shower in 2006

Placing candles at the murder scene of my little sister.

In 2020 with my baby niece R.I.P.

In the year 2013, my two oldest sons

All of my boys in 2020

All of my boys in 2023 with me

Working at Walmart in 2015 as a Customer Service Manager

A Walmart Supervisor in 2016

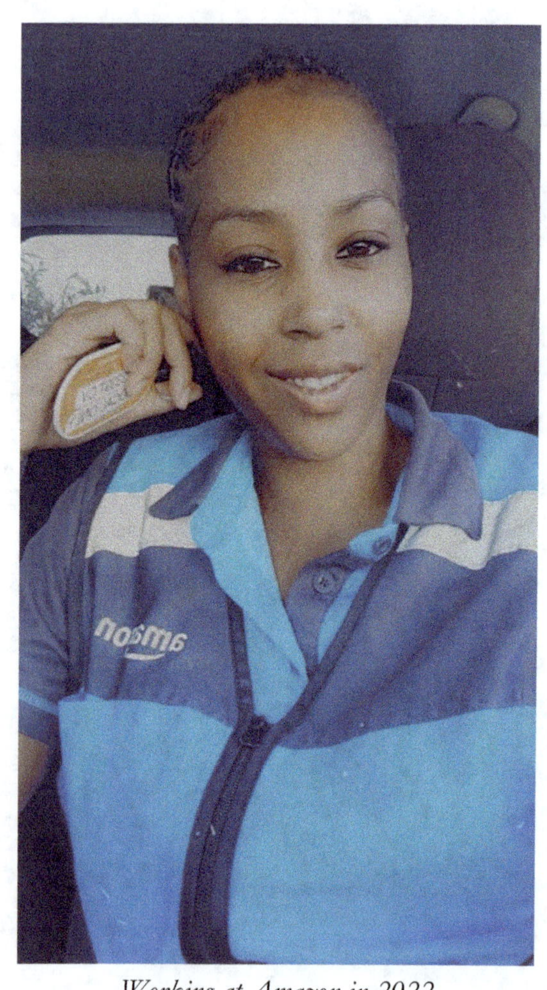

Working at Amazon in 2022

Working on my bingo game in 2022

A focused me in 2022

My first professional photo shoot in 2022

My new Necessary Way product line launched in 2022